HOUGHTON MIFFLIN HARCOURT

PHOTOGRAPHY CREDITS: COVER (bg) ©Ariadne Van Zandbergen/Lonely Planet Images/Getty Images; 3 (b) ©Ariadne Van Zandbergen/Lonely Planet Images/Getty Images; 4 (t) ©Reed Kaestner/Corbis; 5 (b) ©Zhabska Tetyana/Shutterstock; 6 (b) ©EcoPrint/Shutterstock; 7 (t) ©Dave Strickland/Shutterstock; 8 (t) ©DLILLC/Corbis; 9 (b) ©Brian J. Skerry/National Geographic/Getty Images; 10 (t) ©Dr. Morley Read/Shutterstock; 11 (b) ©PM Images/Stone/Getty Images; 12 (b) ©Tier Und Naturfotografie J und C Sohn/Photographer's Choice/Getty Images; 13 (t) ©Ocean/Corbis; 14 (t) ©TSpider/Shutterstock; 15 (b) ©davidpstephens/Shutterstock; 16 (t) ©Zurijeta/Shutterstock; 17 (tl) ©Image Werks Co., Ltd/Alamy Images; (cl) ©Gregory Bergman/Alamy Images; (bl) ©Stockdisc/Getty Images; (br) ©Marcin Pawinski/Shutterstock; (cr) ©Gerry Ellis/Digital Vision/Getty Images; (tr) ©Creatas/Getty Images; 18 (b) ©PhotoDisc/Getty Images; 20 (b) ©photodisc/Getty Images; 21 (t) ©Radius Images/Alamy Images

Printed in China

ISBN: 978-0-544-07310-4

14 15 16 17 0940 20 19 18 17

4500693654 A B C D E F G

Be an Active Reader!

Look for each word in yellow along with its meaning.

nutrients	consumer	decomposer
energy	herbivore	food chain
producer	carnivore	food web
photosynthesis	omnivore	

Underlined sentences answer the questions.

What do all living things need?
How do plants make food?
What is a consumer?
What is a herbivore?
What is a carnivore?
What is an omnivore?
What is a scavenger?
What is a decomposer?
What is the predator/prey relationship?
How does energy move through a food chain?
What is a food web?
How do changes in an ecosystem affect a food web?

What do all living things need?

All living things need nutrients. Nutrients help living things grow and stay healthy. Plants get the nutrients they need from the soil. Animals get nutrients from the food they eat. All living things also need energy. Energy is the ability to cause changes in matter. Living things get nutrients and energy from their environment.

How many kinds of living things do you see in this picture?

How do plants make food?

Green plants use energy from the sun to make their own food.

Plants are producers. A producer is a living thing that can make its own food. Plants make their own food by photosynthesis. Photosynthesis is the process in which plants use energy from the sun to change carbon dioxide and water into sugar and oxygen.

Photosynthesis takes place mostly in plant leaves. The leaves contain a green substance called chlorophyll. The chlorophyll traps the sunlight.

The plant's roots soak up water and nutrients from the soil. The plant's leaves take in carbon dioxide. This is a gas. Plants give off oxygen. Humans and animals need oxygen to breathe.

Plants make sugar. The sugar stays in the plant's roots, stems, and leaves. The plant needs the sugars to stay alive. Photosynthesis takes place over and over. Without it, the plant will die.

Without plants, there would be less oxygen in the environment. There would be more carbon dioxide. We could not live.

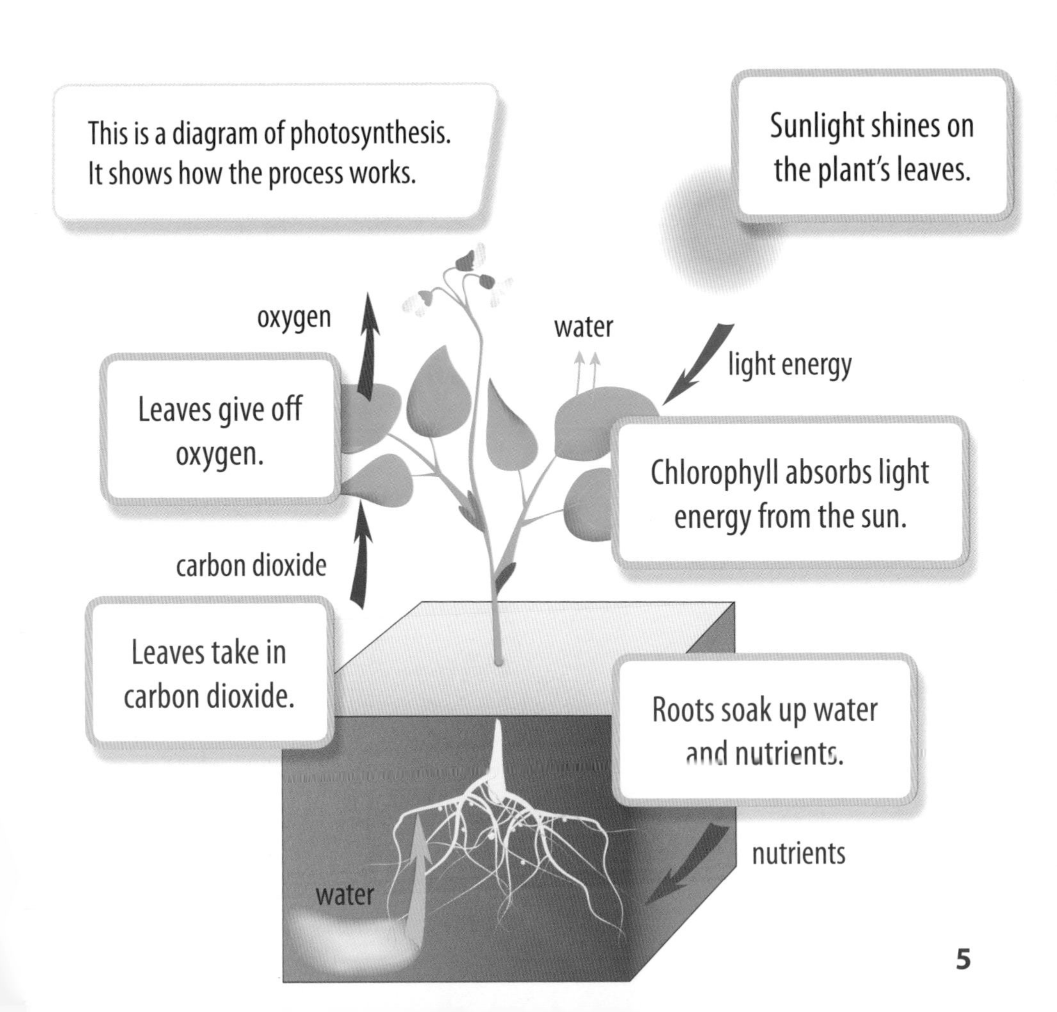

What is a consumer?

A consumer is an animal that eats plants or other animals to get energy. Consumers can't make their own food. They get their food from other sources.

The food that a consumer eats depends on where it lives. Different consumers may eat the same food. There may be a lot of consumers, but not much food. Some consumers will not have enough to eat. There may be a lot of food for a type of consumer. The numbers of that type of consumer will grow. Eventually there will be too many consumers for the food available.

Some consumers eat other consumers. A beetle eats a leaf from a plant. The beetle is a consumer. A small bird eats the beetle. A weasel eats the bird. A fox eats the weasel. The chart below shows some consumers. It shows what the consumers eat. It also shows what eats the consumers.

Consumer	What It Eats	What Eats It
red fox	crickets, nuts, mice	bobcats, wolves
bird	seeds, insects	snakes, squirrels
mole	insects	owls, foxes
trout	fish eggs, algae	eagles, otters

What is a herbivore?

A herbivore is an animal that eats only plants or other producers. Many herbivores eat a lot of plants because they need a lot of energy to survive. Some herbivores eat almost all day long, every day! Herbivores come in all sizes. They live in many different environments. Some eat every part of a plant. Others only eat certain parts.

Many forest dwellers are herbivores. Moose and deer are large herbivores. Woodchucks and beavers are smaller herbivores. These animals like the sweet fruit on plants. They strip off tree bark. They munch on grasses, nuts, and twigs. Some forest insects feed on leaves.

Some forest herbivores eat all parts of a plant.

Did you know that some herbivores live in the ocean? Manatees and dugongs are large sea mammals. They have strong snouts and rough lips. They pull up sea grasses and weeds. Green sea turtles eat algae. Parrotfish and unicorn fish also eat algae. Shrimp and crabs eat algae, too.

Some herbivores live in the desert. Kangaroo rats and mice eat mostly seeds. But they will also eat all parts of a cactus plant. They will eat the spiny outside, tender fruit, and the juicy inside. Tiny ants and beetles also eat cactus. Quail are desert birds. They eat cactus seeds and fruit. Bighorn sheep and burros like to eat brush and grasses.

Manatees live in warm coastal waters. They eat the plants they find in the water.

What is a carnivore?

Carnivores must catch their meals.

A carnivore is an animal that only eats other animals. Carnivores hunt for their food. They may have sharp teeth and powerful jaws. These features help them chew meat. Hunting takes a lot of energy. Carnivores need to eat a lot to have enough energy.

Rain forests have many carnivores. Large harpy eagles catch smaller birds. Jaguars are large cats that hunt birds and smaller mammals. Huge anaconda snakes eat rats and frogs. Anacondas can also eat crocodiles! Piranhas are fish that eat smaller fish. The praying mantis is an insect. It is also a carnivore. It eats beetles and other insects.

Large and small carnivores live in the ocean. The great white shark is one of the best-known carnivores. It eats mostly seals and sea lions. Blue whales eat tons of tiny marine animals called krill. Toothed whales also eat shrimp, fish, and penguins. Some fish eat other fish. Octopuses and walruses eat other marine animals.

Carnivores also live in the Arctic. Polar bears eat ringed seals. They eat whales and birds, too. Wolves travel in packs. They hunt caribou. Foxes eat hares and birds. The snowy owl eats small rodents.

The least weasel is a small carnivore. It's only about 25 centimeters (10 inches) long. This hunter lives in forests. It often fights and eats moles and birds. It also eats eggs.

Carnivores that live in water eat other animals that live in water.

What is an omnivore?

An omnivore is an animal that eats both plants and other animals. Forests have many omnivores. A chipmunk's main foods are seeds and nuts. It also eats bugs, eggs, and small lizards. Black bears eat plants and fish. They also eat small mammals and insects.

Baboons live on the grasslands of Africa. They eat plants. They also eat lizards, insects, and birds.

Emus live on the grasslands of Australia. They are large birds. They eat caterpillars. They also eat green plants and seeds.

Peacocks eat insects and flowers. Sometimes they eat reptiles or small mammals.

Omnivores have a large choice of foods. They eat both plants and other animals.

What is a scavenger?

A scavenger is a consumer that eats dead plants and animals. Scavengers have an important job. They remove dead animals and plants from the environment.

Scavengers help clean up the environment.

Opossums, foxes, and coyotes are scavengers. They eat dead animals. Crabs and shrimp eat dead material in the ocean. Cockroaches eat dead plants and animals. California condors, sea gulls, and crows are also scavengers.

Hyenas eat dead animals and plant material. They even eat bones! Packs of jackals often follow hyenas. The jackals eat what hyenas leave behind.

What is a decomposer?

Larger decomposers help break down big pieces of material. Then smaller decomposers break it down even more.

A decomposer is a living thing that gets energy by breaking down wastes and remains of plants and animals. When living things die, they still have nutrients in them. Decomposers help recycle these nutrients. It takes a lot of decomposers to break down a plant or an animal.

Bacteria and fungi are tiny decomposers. There can be a billion of them in a handful of dirt. Earthworms, snails, and slugs are also decomposers. They eat dead material. They leave tiny bits. These bits are easy for the bacteria and fungi to break down.

Crabs and young insects live in water. They are also decomposers. Some bacteria and fungi also live in water.

What is the predator/prey relationship?

A predator is an animal that hunts and kills other animals for food. Prey are the animals a predator eats. Most carnivores are predators. An ecosystem needs predators to stay in balance. Predators eat some of the herbivores. Then there is enough food for the rest of the plant eaters. Predators also eat sick or dying animals. This helps keep the other animals healthy.

Predators have adaptations that help them catch prey. They are often fast. Their eyes and hearing may be sharp. They may have claws to grab their prey.

Many prey have adaptations that help them stay safe. They have hard shells or sharp quills. Some look like twigs or leaves. Others make the predators think they are dead.

The great white shark is one of the top predators in the ocean. No other animal preys on it.

How does energy move through a food chain?

A food chain is the transfer of energy in a sequence of living things. A food chain starts with the sun. The sun gives energy to a producer. There may be one or more consumers in a food chain. A food chain ends with a consumer that no other consumers eat. A food chain usually has two to five links. Each link of the food chain uses energy.

The sun helps watermelons grow. In this case, the watermelon is the producer. A person eats a piece of watermelon. The person is the consumer. This food chain has two links. One link is the watermelon. The other link is the person.

A food chain usually has at least one predator. A predator can become prey for another predator. Look at the food chain below. The sun gives energy to the corn. The corn is the producer. The grasshopper eats a leaf from the corn. The grasshopper is a consumer. The mole is a predator. It eats the grasshopper. The mole becomes prey for the fox. The fox is a predator. Then the fox becomes prey for the eagle. The eagle is the top predator in this food chain.

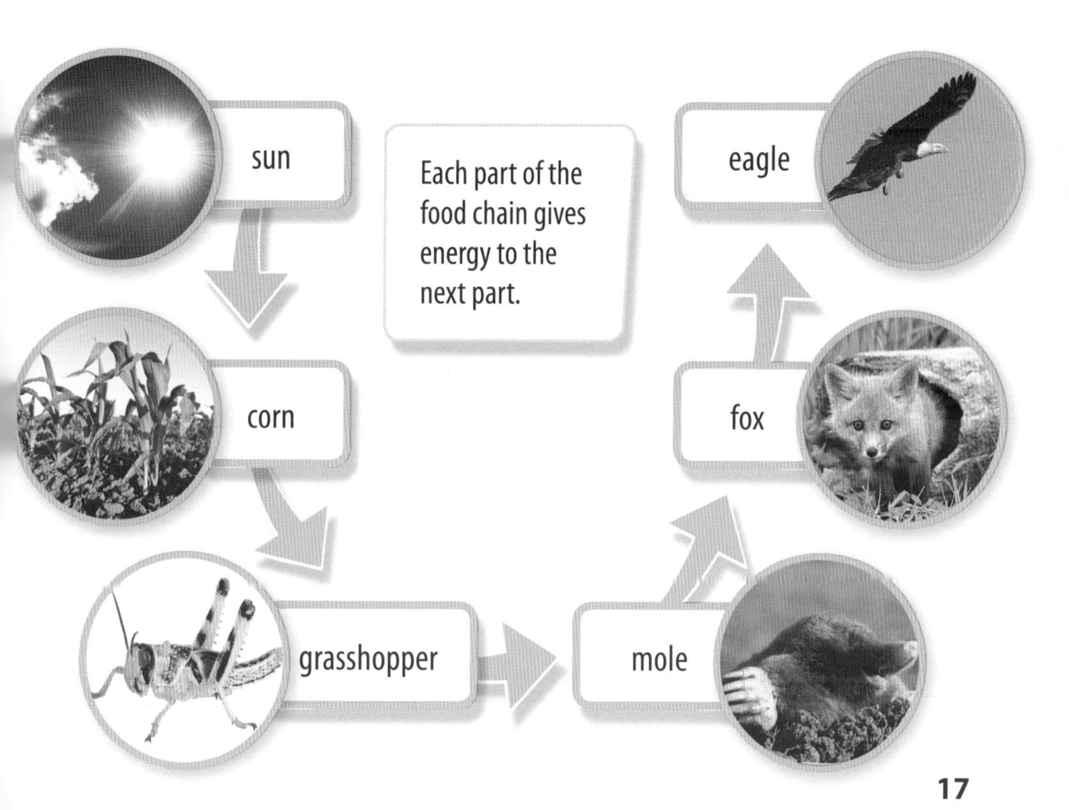

What is a food web?

A food web is a diagram that shows the relationships among different food chains in an ecosystem. Animals often eat more than one food. This means they can be part of more than one food chain. An animal might be part of several food chains. A food web shows these relationships.

The plants and animals in a food web may vary at different times of the year. Some animals move to a different place during winter. Others go to sleep in the winter. Animals that do not move or sleep eat whatever they can find.

Geese migrate. They fly long distances to find food.

This is how a forest food web might look.

The hawk is the main predator and the biggest consumer. It eats rabbits, toads, and even other birds.

The rabbit will be consumed by the hawk. If rabbits were not eaten by hawks, they would eat more plants, which would affect all the other consumers.

The robin and toad get their energy from plants and insects.

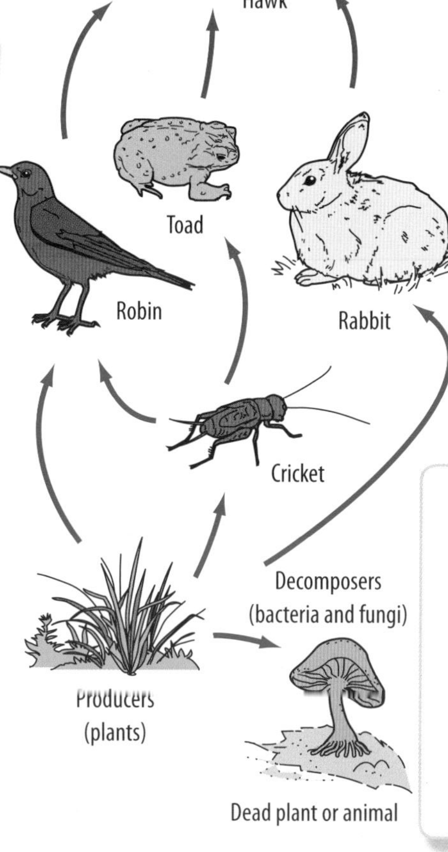

Plants are producers. They use the sun's energy to make their own food.

All of the living things in the food web eventually end up as food for decomposers, which return nutrients to the soil so that the cycle can continue.

How do changes in an ecosystem affect a food web?

Any change in an ecosystem affects its food web. Let's look at a forest. Fire is a natural part of a forest ecosystem. Suppose there's no fire for several years. Rotting wood and leaves build up on the forest floor. Producers such as grasses don't have room to grow. The herbivores might not have enough to eat. Some may move or die. Then carnivores and omnivores won't have enough food. They may also move or die. The forest ecosystem is out of balance.

In this dense forest, some herbivores may have a hard time finding food.

A fire can help the plants and animals in a forest.

Now suppose there's a storm. Lightning hits some of the trees and causes a fire. The fire burns the growth on the forest floor. It may burn some thick sections of the forest, too.

The good news is that forests naturally recover! The ashes from the fire contain nutrients that recycle into the ground. New plants appear. These plants supply more food for the herbivores. The population of herbivores increases. There is more food for the carnivores and omnivores.

When the forest growth is thinner, it's easier for animals to find or build homes. The number of animals increases. There is more food for each link in the food chain. The forest ecosystem is back in balance.

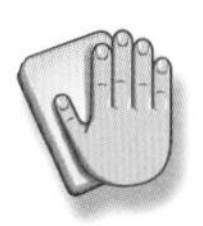

Observe Decomposers

Watch decomposers at work! Ask an adult for a small piece of bread, fruit, or vegetable. Use a cotton swab to put some dust or dirt on one part of the food. Put a few drops of water on another part of the food. Put the food in a small plastic bag. Then close the bag tightly. Look at the food every day for a week or two. Notice the changes. Do not open the bag or touch the food with your hands.

Draw a Picture

Use the Internet to find out ways in which forest fires help a forest ecosystem. Choose one way and draw a picture showing it. Add labels to your picture and write a paragraph to go along with your drawing. Be sure your paragraph explains the way in which a forest is helped.

Glossary

carnivore [KAHR•nuh•vawr] A consumer that eats only other animals. *A great white shark is a carnivore.*

consumer [kuhn•SOOM•er] An animal that eats plants or other animals to get energy. *Rabbits are consumers that eat plants.*

decomposer [dee•kuhm•POHZ•er] A living thing that gets energy by breaking down wastes and the remains of plants and animals. *An earthworm is a decomposer that crawls through the soil.*

energy [EN•er•jee] The ability to do work and cause changes in matter. *Energy from the sun helps plants grow.*

food chain [FOOD CHAYN] The transfer of food energy in a sequence of living things. *A plant is at the beginning of every food chain.*

food web [FOOD WEB] A diagram that shows the relationship among different food chains in an ecosystem. *A food web for the ocean might include algae, small fish, large fish, and a shark.*

herbivore [HER•buh•vawr] An animal that eats only plants or other producers. *A cow is an herbivore that eats grass.*

nutrient [NOO•tree•uhnt] A material used by living things for growth and for other life functions. *The plant gets nutrients through its roots in the soil.*

omnivore [AHM•nih•vawr] A consumer that eats both plants and other animals. *An emu is an omnivore that eats insects and seeds.*

photosynthesis [foht•oh•SIN•thuh•sis] The process in which plants use energy from the sun to change carbon dioxide and water into sugar and oxygen. *Photosynthesis takes place when there is enough sunshine.*

producer [pruh•DOOS•er] A living thing, such as a plant, that can make its own food. *Vegetables and fruits are producers.*